MW01676329

Wor[illegible] Ants

by Chana Stiefel

HOUGHTON MIFFLIN HARCOURT
School Publishers

PHOTOGRAPHY CREDITS: Cover © age fotostock/SuperStock. 1 ImageState/Alamy. 2 ImageState/Alamy. 3 Ted Clutter/ Photo Researchers, Inc. 8 © age fotostock/SuperStock. 9 © Tom Brakefield/CORBIS. 10 Roger Eritja/Alamy.

Copyright © by Houghton Mifflin Harcourt Publishing Company

All rights reserved. No part of this work may be reproduced or transmitted in any form or by any means, electronic or mechanical, including photocopying or recording, or by any information storage and retrieval system, without the prior written permission of the copyright owner unless such copying is expressly permitted by federal copyright law. Requests for permission to make copies of any part of the work should be addressed to Houghton Mifflin Harcourt School Publishers, Attn: Permissions, 6277 Sea Harbor Drive, Orlando, Florida 32887-6777.

Printed in China

ISBN-13: 978-0-547-02174-4
ISBN-10: 0-547-02174-7

2 3 4 5 6 7 8 0940 18 17 16 15 14 13 12 11 10

If you have received these materials as examination copies free of charge, Houghton Mifflin Harcourt School Publishers retains title to the materials and they may not be resold. Resale of examination copies is strictly prohibited.

Possession of this publication in print format does not entitle users to convert this publication, or any portion of it, into electronic format.

Introduction

Have you ever seen ants at a picnic? They crawl all over. They scout out food. Then they carry it back to their nest.

Ants are tiny but amazing insects. In fact, they are a lot like us. They live and work in groups. They gather and store food. Ants also take care of each other. To find out more about these busy bugs, dig in!

Ants work together to collect food.

Ants All Around

Ants have lived on Earth for more than 100 million years! Today, more than 12,000 kinds of ants live all over the world. The puzzling thing is that they don't live in Antarctica. Just kidding! It makes a lot of sense that ants don't live there. It's way too cold. Ants prefer warmer places.

Carpenter ants dig tunnels in wood.

Ant Family

Ants live in a group called a colony. Every member of the colony has a job. The queen is the mother of all of the ants in the colony. Some queens can lay millions of eggs each year.

Worker ants are also female, but they don't lay eggs. They do all the chores. They dig and clean the nest. They watch over the eggs. They also find food and protect the colony. The workers live for one to three years.

Male ants have one job: to mate with the queen. The males live for only a few weeks.

Ant Life Cycle

The queen digs a hole in the ground and lays eggs.

The eggs develop into larvae.

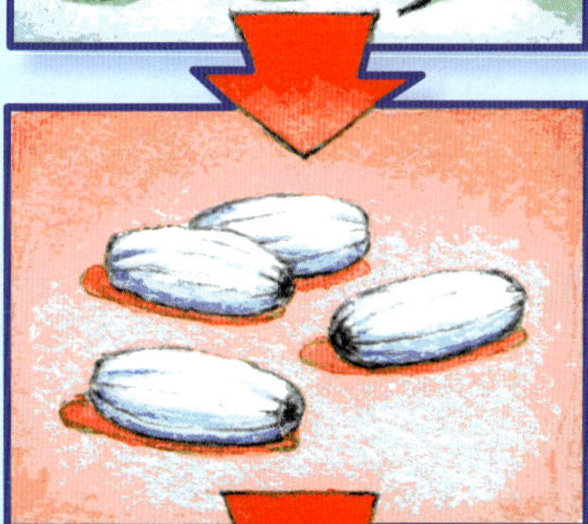

The larvae develop into pupae.

An adult ant hatches out of each pupa.

Ant Colony

A small ant colony may have only a few ants, but large colonies may be home to millions of ants. Some ants live inside plants or tree trunks, but most ants live underground. They dig narrow tunnels with their jaws. As they carry out the dirt, they build an anthill.

The ant nest lies under an anthill. Ants dig their nests in soggy earth so their bodies don't dry out. Nests have many rooms, called chambers. The queen lays eggs in some of these chambers, and workers also store food here.

An ant colony is a busy place.

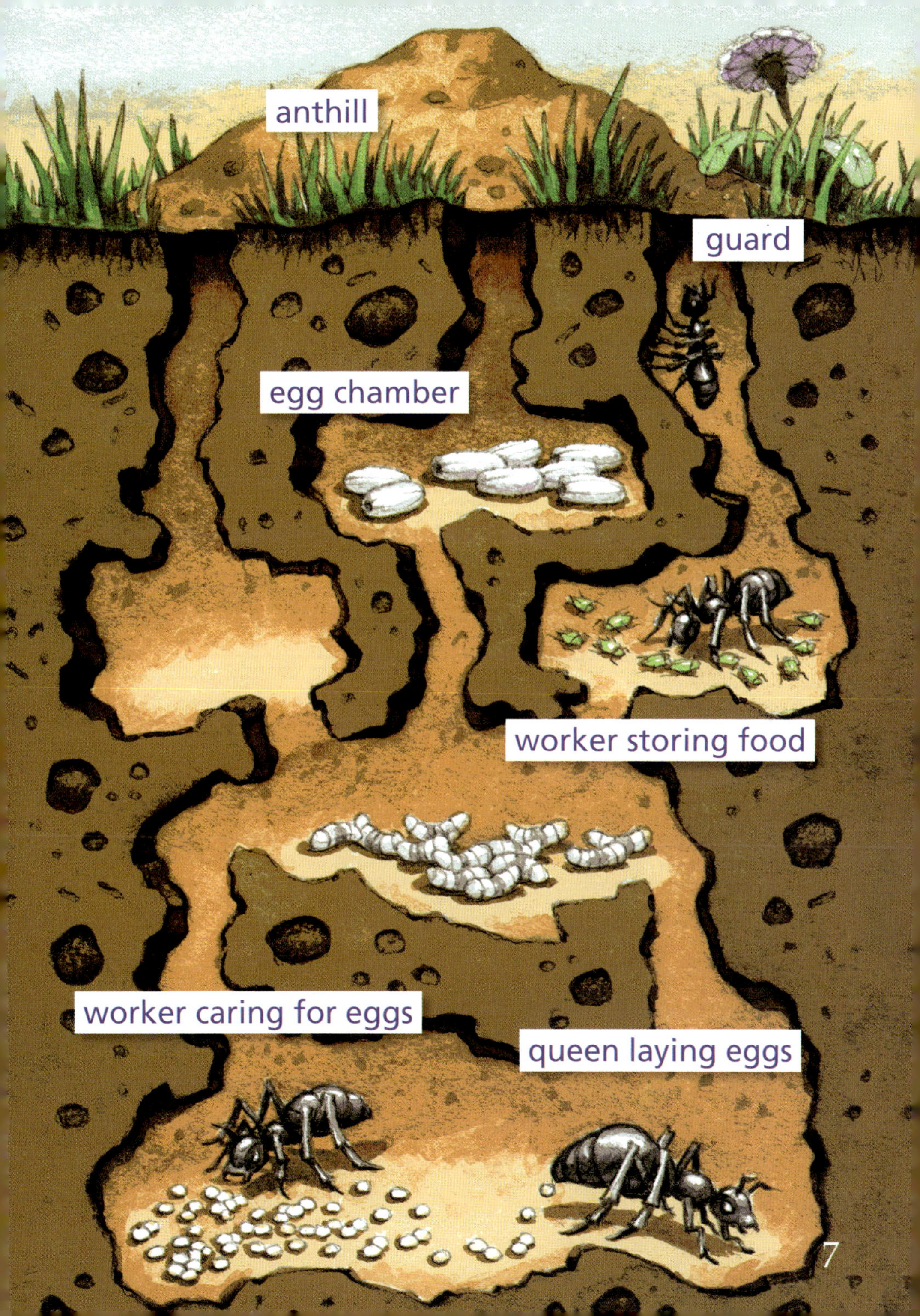
anthill
guard
egg chamber
worker storing food
worker caring for eggs
queen laying eggs

Feed Me!

Most ants like sweets. Sugar gives them energy. When an ant finds food, it goes back to the nest to alert others. The ant leaves a smelly trail so other ants can find the food. The ants pick up the smell using their long antennae, or feelers. Soon the food is surrounded by lots of ants.

Some ants drink a liquid sugar called honeydew. This glassy liquid is made by other insects.

Tiny insects called aphids make a liquid sugar called honeydew. Ants collect honeydew from the aphids.

Danger!

Ants have many enemies. A giant anteater uses sharp claws to violently tear open an ant nest. Its long, sticky tongue can lap up 20,000 ants in one meal! Lizards, frogs, birds, and bears also try to catch ants unaware. Yet many ants fight back. For example, fire ants bite and sting.

The giant anteater can grow up to seven feet long. It feasts on ants.

The next time you see an anthill, watch closely. Drop a crumb and study the ants in action. See how they work together. What can we learn from tiny ants?

How is an ant colony like a city of people?

Responding

TARGET VOCABULARY Word Builder

Make a word web around the word scout. What other words mean the same thing? Copy this web and add more words.

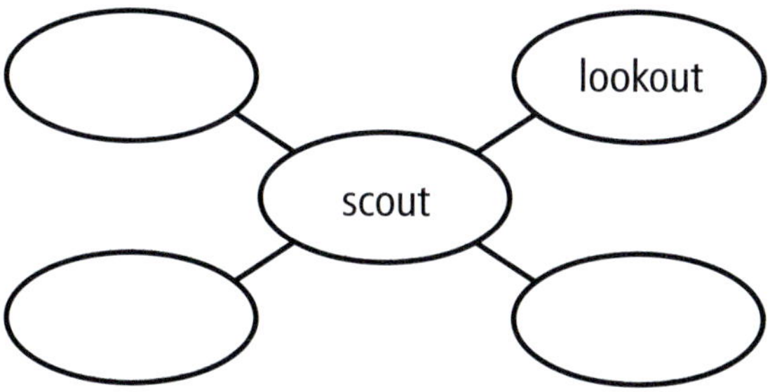

Write About It

Text to Text Ant colonies use scouts to find food. Write about another animal colony you've read about and tell about the animals that live in the colony, their different jobs, and how they all work together. Use words from the word web in your writing.

TARGET VOCABULARY

glassy	**soggy**
liquid	**surrounded**
narrow	**unaware**
puzzling	**underground**
scout	**violently**

TARGET STRATEGY **Monitor/Clarify** As you read, find a way to clear up what doesn't make sense.

Word Teaser Drop the *-y* and you drink out of it.